In memory of
Avraham Hanoch Levy (Lev) Angel
May 2006 – December 2016

A kind-natured and curious boy who loved this world with the purest heart,
and with a love of truth, sought to question and understand everything.

AnnabelleAndAiden.com

For FREE BOOK GIVEAWAYS and news, 'like' us at Facebook.com/AnnabelleAndAiden

Annabelle and Aiden
gazed at the sky.
At moons and stars
and comets so high.

"Wow!" Aiden said,
almost dropping his drink.
Annabelle stared
and started to think.

"How'd they get there,
these moons and rocks,
scattered above us
like so many dots?"

3

Aiden shrugged, "They must've come
when people came along.
I feel they're here just for us;
my feelings can't be wrong."

"Ha-ha-ha," the children heard,
"The name's Tardigrade Tom.
They've been here the whole time, long
before your great grandmom.
great
great
great
great

"You just showed up! The stars and I,
so long we've had to wait
to show you all the stuff you missed.
I figured you'd be late!"

4

THE UNIVERSE, and all within it is about 13.8 billion years old, and us humans have been here about 0.00146% of that time (and are only able to live in less than 0.000000000000000000003% of its space, or about 13.31% of the Earth's surface.) By anyone's standards, it seems to not entirely want us here. And we just recently showed up!

TARDIGRADES (or "water bears"), on the other hand, have been here for 600 million years (at least two thousand times more than humans have) and are known as the world's toughest animal: they can (and do) live everywhere, from boiling water to outer space. They've been around far longer than us. If the universe was made for anyone, one might quip it was made for tardigrades like Tom.

Aiden said, "I'll hear their tale,
but they make me feel small.
The world's so big! How could we know
if we matter at all?"

The distance to the edge of the observable universe
is about 46 billion light years (and expanding by the minute!)

6

"Well," Tom said, "before it grew, the whole world was smaller than... you!"

A long time ago,
there was diddly-squat.
Just nothing at all,
except... one tiny dot.

Can you find it?

What is Nothing? (And is it something?) It hurts our heads to think about, so much that the Greeks (who despised the idea) refused to incorporate zero into their numbers, but let's try. Is Nothing dark empty space? No, that has particles. Radiation. Gravity. What if we took those away? One may think so, but the maximally empty space is in fact not empty at all. It has shape. Topology, even. Some physicists describe a genuine Nothing, void of space, time, particles, field, and laws of nature. Mathematicians have proposed starting with a set of numbers that includes only the number zero, and then removing zero. We still can't agree on exactly what Nothing is, but we do have several propositions to start with. And, well, that may be something (about Nothing).

10

All the stuff in the world,
everything you've ever seen,
from juggling bears to monkey hairs,
and every jelly bean...

and mops and cops
and baseball bats,
my favorite socks,
Ms. Reynold's cats

were squeezed and squished
and mashed and mushed
into that dot,
into that spot.

*Don't be
so dense!*

11

Small, but so heavy
like millions of gifts
wrapped up in hippos
that no one could lift.

It got so squished,
it needed more room.
So it pushed and it pushed
and it (sort of) went...

What happened before (or "caused") the big bang?
The short answer is, we just don't know. Some physicists will say the
very question is wrong: though it hurts our tiny brains to think
about, there was no "before" the big bang at all: time itself did not
exist! (Since neither did space; there was only Nothing.)
Others may tell you that our big bang was not the first, but rather
one of many, as our universe continues to expand, then contract into a
tiny dot, and then expand again ad infinitum. But again, we simply
don't know. Which, perhaps, for the scientific mind, is the most
exciting thing of all.

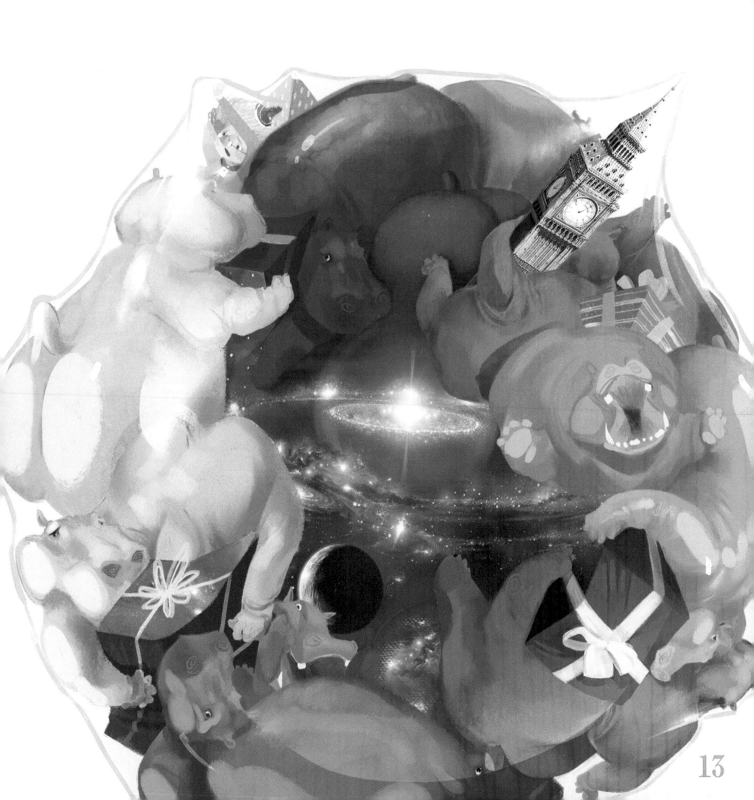

BOOM!

Or bang? I'd call it
a great expansion.
Like Hilbert's balloons at
his hotel mansion.

How do we know? Edwin Hubble saw that the universe is expanding. So, if we simply rewind that process, we get to a universe that expanded from a tiny (dense) point, through an event jokingly named the big bang. And today we see old galaxies forming exactly as they would (and ours has) if sputtered out by a big bang. Also, a telescope near the south pole has detected ripples in spacetime (previously predicted to be) left over from the big bang. Finally, the static you hear on your TV is (in part) sound from the big bang (or specifically, leftover microwave radiation, that's in the room you're in right now). That's right. You can hear the big bang through your TV.

In just one second
quarks turn to stuff
like protons and neutrons
that are just enough

for hydrogen atoms,
in millions of years,
to form gases and dust
as the burning heat clears.

Stars are born
babies, just like us.
They live their lives,
then die without fuss.

They fall apart,
and come together,
forming planets like Earth,
with crazy weather.

18

And from the Earth,
come you and me.
We're made of stars!
Now can't you see?

19

Aiden says, "Great! But I do have to say, all of those stars seem so far away..."

"Oh, but they're in us!
Our bones and our skin.
And even those rocks
you're now sitting in.

You're feeling the stuff
from the bodies of folks
who lived long ago
and stood like great oaks.

And also the people
who have yet to be.
They'll come from our bones,
these rocks and those trees.

21

Every person is made of about 7,000,000,000,000,000,000,000,000,000 atoms! 98% of them are replaced each year. Every person contains DNA long enough to make 140 trips to the sun.

22

And all of us come
from the same exact place:
the Earth, which came from
the stars out in space,

who were kind enough
to explode into shards
that joined to make up
everything that we are.

So when you feel small,
that you don't matter much,
know stars are inside you,
whole worlds you can touch.

Did you know you hold the strength
of hydrogen bombs?
Or that there's parts of different stars
in each of your palms?

24

You're made of pieces
that used to be part
of dinosaurs, Shakespeare,
or Amelia Earhart.

You are the world
experiencing itself.
So do not feel small,
or left on a shelf.

We're made of our world,
its mountains and wells.
So the way that we treat it,
is how we treat ourselves.

There's
WORLDS WITHIN US
you would not believe;
everyone that was
and that ever will be...

are all within you,
and came from the stars.
And that's just how big
and amazing you are.

A special thanks to:

Etta Black, Mandy Wultsch, Rowan & Zoe Curtis and Family, Asher Ward, Melanie Ward, Emily Levin Christensen, Angela Van Raaphorst, Eric Isfeld, Odyssey Rose, O'Neill-Coronado, Kieran Matthew Zico Wood, Efraim Miller, Darcey Isabella Gaudern Smith, Marin Bea Shear, Samuel D. T. Shear, Shayan Aidan Ahmed, Eshaan Zaidan Ahmed, Harri Arnold, Adeline Schwain Finke, Ramona Price, Nieve Sheerin, Julie Lee, Ruth Freeman, Abigail Langston, Henri Dobbin, Noor Pedram, Naya Pedram , Julie Daellenbach, Christopher Port, Dovid, Tali, & Noa Becker, Micheal A Donaghie, Mitul Thobhani, Bellacine Wysk, William, James & Charlie Hude, Milo Maxwell Francois Vettel-Iden, Kara Browne, Autumn Burnlar-White, Molly Elizabeth Kroyer, Landon and Hazel Murphy, Nickol Dameron, Rosie Moxham, Cara Chiu, Jennifer Erdin, Ben Erdin, Jonathan Eric Tornabe, Jordan Evan Tornabe, Jasmine Eden Tornabe, Katia Freedman, Elijah Reader, K. Amber Kreis, Anita Phagan, Iona Baver, Liam Thomas Kott, Shawn Castrapel, Max Castrapel, Diurys, Nicholas Zeidman, Astrid Hatfield-Ladd, Alexis Grayham, Maddox Sheehan, Amber Kaur Gill, Suhani Dhaliwal Gill, Billy Jarvis, Ichiro Kai Burleson, Sydney Burnett, Micah & Olivia Nordlund, Alexandra Peters, Ally Lombardo, Jack Downs, Paul Matteson, Aunt Diane, Ariana Grace Cooke, Delia Ettere, Eloise Stasha, Sophia Far, Paul Taggart, Nicola Taggart, Emma Jade Akerman, Natalie Kaye Akerman, Jackson, Sharon and Jake, Jessica and Dodge Sproviero, Annabelle Moore, Shannon Allen, Kimon C Gonis, Chloe Leigh Rebisz, Derek and Melissa Turnock, Abigail & Selah, Liam Evaul, Tory Evaul, Mark Evaul, SofÃ¬a Tomas Elena, Hongwoo Lee, Yunmi Lee, Loha Lee, Roun Lee, Owen Thomas, Amelia Elidi Nguyen, Henry Coffman, Ethan Michael Thompson, Adelaine Cadence Brewer, Persephone Soleil, Taylor and Osiris Lucian Taylor, April Mariska, Zoe Soleil, Quentin Eliot Davis, Lucas Arun Getzel-Trevick, Penelope Arjuna Getzel-Trevick, Harry Ezra Trevick, Naomi Ruth Trevick, Hailey Palmer, Wyatt Palmer, Cameron Palmer, Kristen Birks, Matthew N.H Pham, alvadua@hotmail.com, Adalyn M, Eleanor D, Eleanor Satomi Gomez, Ben Atlas Wolber, Mei Krause, Ella Violet Pancoast, Jane Foster, Kaija Szumylo, Drew Boswell, John Boswell, Lucy Wagnild, Ali King, Megan Sinclair, Daisy Arya, Lilly Arya, Farhad & Aliyah Khan, Lincoln Simms, Alexander Graham & Maia Graham, Torunn Marguerite Carlson, Teague Freyr Carlson, Natalie Lo, Cillian Wolf Christie, Nila Granillo and Eli Granillo, Maggie Kulzer, Aiden Curtis-Frank Jones, Mary K. Metz, Annabelle Liliana Alpisa, Brett Soltz, Tim Belczak, Samuel Arthur Gen Cooper-Ewing, August Ewing Youngs and Harvey Mac Youngs, Pigrunner, Addison Mai, Gloria Chiu and Stephen Co, Pfarr-Porter Family, Thomas and Annabelle's Dad, Carlyle Mac Sherstad, Ella Maddox Anderson, Amy Burrows, Senor Guapo, Corwin Anthony Senatore, Olivotto Family, Na'amah Rosenzweig & Ellah Rosenzweig, The Espeys, Annabelle Warminski, Amee and Annabelle Hanke, Sam Lewin

CPSIA information can be obtained
at www.ICGtesting.com
Printed in the USA
JSHW050953170423
40394JS00002B/35